HEALTH EDUCATION AUTHORITY

MENTAL HEALTH
PROMOTION
A QUALITY FRAMEWORK

ISBN 0 7521 1042 X

© Health Education Authority, 1997

Health Education Authority
Hamilton House
Mabledon Place
London
WC1H 9TX

Designed by XAB Design

Printed in Great Britain

4

MENTAL HEALTH
P R O M O T I O N
A QUALITY FRAMEWORK

CONTENTS

ACKNOWLEDGEMENT

Many people have contributed time and expertise to the development of this project. This document is the result of wide spread consultation with commissioners and providers in mental health promotion. We would like to thank SHEPS (Society for Health Education and Promotion Specialists) who have allowed us full access to their mental health work which helped to shape some of our thinking. We would also particularly like to thank the project's independent advisory group, those who attended the consultation events in 1996 and all those who were involved in the piloting process – individuals who were involved in the evaluation research and those who completed their feedback forms. Also, Laurann Yen, for her facilitation and writing skills, Mary Hainge for her incisive research report which has enabled us to improve the final document and colleagues at the HEA, particularly Jane Lethbridge and Anna Grey for their advice and support.

We still welcome feedback on the document, which we hope will be a practical tool for commissioners and providers of mental health promotion, to develop strategies, based on sound evidence of effectiveness, using good practice and measuring the results.

Elizabeth Gale
Project Manager
Health Education Authority

Although there is a growing body of evidence that mental health is fundamental to positive health and well-being, mental health promotion remains the most under-developed area of health promotion. Mental health promotion acknowledges the importance of the mind and emotions. How we think, feel and communicate affects our experiences at all levels - in the family, in the workplace and in the community. Mental health is just as important as physical health and yet there are few examples of strategies for the planning and delivery of mental health promotion.

In the early stages of this project, it became clear that many professionals in all sectors are committed to mental health promotion, but there are two key barriers to developing a strategic approach to mental health. These are a lack of information on effectiveness, and the difficulty of evaluating mental health promotion initiatives. In addition, although there is an increasing recognition of the social and economic costs of mental illness, the costs and consequences of failing to promote mental health are difficult to quantify.

This document provides a framework for demonstrating the benefits and value of mental health promotion, with a key focus on measuring success. Although there is clearly an ongoing need for more research, it argues that there is sufficient evidence to justify investing resources in mental health promotion. For both commissioners and practitioners, this guide provides a starting point for identifying priorities and planning interventions in areas which are known to be effective.

Many agencies have a role to play in promoting the capacity for mental health in a wide range of settings, at a variety of levels. Mental health promotion is certainly not confined to a health setting alone. This quality framework has been developed to highlight the potential for mental health promotion with individuals and in the social, economic and organisational environment. It also demonstrates the importance of a mental health perspective on structural barriers to health. This resource is intended to be of value to colleagues working in all sectors, as well as those with a specific remit for mental health.

In addition to the challenges of evaluation and effectiveness addressed in this text, there is a further problem for mental health promotion. Mental health is an area which is deeply tabooed. The stigma surrounding mental health problems contributes greatly to the suffering of those experiencing mental distress, their friends, families and carers. It may prevent people from seeking help and also inhibits organisations from developing mental health policies, notably in the workplace. Mental health promotion, therefore, has a key role to play in reducing fear and anxiety and changing attitudes and awareness, in an area that is crucial to the achievement of positive health.

Dr Lynne Friedli
Account Manager
Health Education Authority

This guide

- introduces mental health promotion and makes the case for *investment* in mental health promotion
- looks at what makes *good mental health* more likely, and what makes it less likely
- reviews the *effectiveness* of current mental health promotion activities
- sets out a *strategy* for developing a quality framework for mental health promotion
- shows how to use *indicators* to measure the effectiveness of mental health promotion

You should read it if you are:

- a *commissioner* wanting to decide about where to invest effectively in mental health promotion
- a *provider* wanting to develop and deliver good mental health promotion activities
- a *member of a group* promoting mental health
- *interested* in developing the thinking and practice around mental health promotion

WHAT DO I DO WITH IT AND HOW CAN I USE IT?

The guide provides a quality framework for mental health promotion.

The framework will enable you to develop a strategy for mental health promotion through:

- defining the remit for mental health promotion in your area

- defining the mental health needs of the community which you aim to serve

- identifying effective interventions, for a range of target groups

- planning strategically to ensure that the programme is delivered through inter-disciplinary and multi-agency working, across all sectors and at all levels

- developing appropriate indicators to measure the inputs, impacts and outcomes of the programme

- effectively evaluating the programme developed, within a cycle of review and audit

- establishing good practice in the process of planning and delivering mental health promotion

'Mental health underpins all facets of our existence. It is essential to our ability to perceive, comprehend and interpret our surroundings, to think and speak, and to communicate with each other verbally and non-verbally. It is essential to our capacity to form and sustain relationships, and to pursue our daily lives in the various societies and cultures in which we live.' (Jenkins, unpublished, 1997)

Good mental health is the product of a complex set of factors, and many agencies in all sectors have the potential and the opportunity to promote mental health, at a variety of levels.

Mental health is promoted through a number of avenues including:

- *public policy and structural approaches:* addressing issues known to affect mental health, for example, unemployment, poverty, inequality, social exclusion, housing, public safety, racism and discrimination
- *health promotion and education:* which might include exercise, coping skills, parenting skills, relationship skills, negotiating and self-assertion techniques, opportunities for participation and social inclusion and programmes to build self-esteem
- *work directed at the primary prevention of mental illness:* such as social support for new mothers, reducing the rate of post natal depression
- *improving the quality of life* of people experiencing mental distress

Mental health promotion has significant potential to contribute to the Government's new public health agenda, notably in areas such as community participation, social exclusion and emotional literacy. Mental health promotion will also contribute to and benefit from the Government's broader priorities for action, such as tackling unemployment, particularly among the young, the provision of adequate housing and high quality pre-school education.

Improving the mental health of individuals, families, organisations and communities has a number of recognised benefits. It:

- improves physical health
- increases emotional resilience, enabling people to enjoy life and to survive difficulties and distress
- enhances citizenship, giving people the skills and confidence to adopt meaningful and effective roles in society
- increases productivity

Mental health promotion, therefore, has a number of benefits:

- promoting mental health may help to reduce either the incidence or the severity of mental health problems
- mental health problems account for significant costs for individuals, their families, their employers, the health service and the country as a whole, which may be reduced by effective mental health promotion
- there is a moral argument that the promotion of mental health is worthwhile in itself, and that it is a basic community responsibility to foster mental as well as physical well being

The benefits of mental health promotion enable us to make the case for further investment. This case needs to be viewed within the context of the current incidence, severity and cost of mental health problems in this country.

Incidence

- At the current time 1 in 7 people experiences a mental health problem and this rate appears to be directly affected by various social factors including:

  - unemployment (rates up to 100 per cent higher),
  - being a lone parent or living alone (rates are between 26–80 per cent higher),
  - living in rented accommodation, particularly from local authorities and housing associations (rates are up to 50 per cent higher) and
  - living in urban areas (rates are between 20–40 per cent higher)
    (OPCS Survey (1995): *The prevalence of psychiatric morbidity among adults living in private households*)

- It is estimated that 1 in 4 adults in any one year will experience some form of mental health problem.
  (Goldberg, Filters to care – model (1991), In Jenkins, R and Griffiths, S. *Indicators for mental health in the population*)

- In 1995 there were 3,579 suicides recorded by coroners in England and Wales – this is almost 10 deaths a day. Suicide rates are higher among men and higher still among the unemployed.
  (Home Office, *Statistical Bulletin* (April, 1996). Government Statistical Service: *Statistics of deaths reported to coroners: England and Wales*)

Costs

- It is estimated that the cost of mental health problems for 1996–97 will total over £32 billion.
  (Knapp, M.K. and Patel, A. (1997). The cost of mental health – unpublished).

- In 1992/93, NHS expenditure on mental health services totalled almost £1.93 billion – inpatient expenditure was the majority of this cost at £1.78 billion (14.6 per cent of total inpatient costs) and outpatient expenditure accounted for £154.6 million (6.7 per cent of total outpatient costs).
  (NHS Executive (1996a). *Burdens of disease*)

- In 1993, over £201.4 million was spent on medication for mental health problems.
  (Department of Health (1996) – *Statistics of prescription dispensed in FHSAs, England 1985–95*)
  Between 1994 and 1995 the number of anti-depressant prescriptions rose by 12 per cent with an increase in medication costs of 25 per cent.
  (Knapp, M.K. and Patel, A. (1997). The cost of mental health – unpublished)

- The local authority personal social services net expenditure for mental illness in 1994–95 totalled £311 million in England.
  (Department of Health (1996). *Health and social services statistics for England*)

- It is estimated that 80 million working days are lost per year due to anxiety and depression, at a cost of £5.3 billion.
  (Confederation of British Industry and Department of Health (1992). *Promoting mental health at work*)
  Also, stress related absences account for half of all sicknesses costing a further £4 billion.
  (Cooper, C. and Cartwright, S. (1996). *Mental health and stress in the workplace*)

- Over 167,000 spells of certified absence in 1994–95 were reported due to mental health problems and there were over 306,000 claimants for invalidity benefits.
  (Social security statistics (1996))

- Informal carers, if paid, would require a total annual budget of over £2.83 billion.
  (Nuttal, S.R. *et al* (1993). *Financing long term care in Great Britain*. Institute of Actuaries)

Some of the official figures above are considered to be underestimates – this is largely due to the stigma which surrounds mental health problems. This is true particularly for certified absence statistics and recorded suicide rates.

Further information on the global burden of mental health problems is described in Jenkins, R 'Nations for mental health', in *Social psychiatry and psychiatric epidemiology* (1997) **32:**309-311.

The Quality Framework for Mental Health Promotion is developed in the context of the broad determinants of health and mental health, and within the scope of mental health promotion.

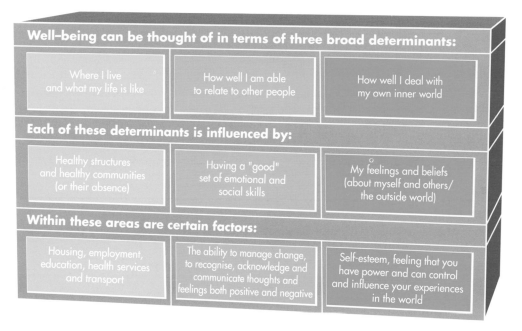

Well–being can be thought of in terms of three broad determinants:

| Where I live and what my life is like | How well I am able to relate to other people | How well I deal with my own inner world |

Each of these determinants is influenced by:

| Healthy structures and healthy communities (or their absence) | Having a "good" set of emotional and social skills | My feelings and beliefs (about myself and others/ the outside world) |

Within these areas are certain factors:

| Housing, employment, education, health services and transport | The ability to manage change, to recognise, acknowledge and communicate thoughts and feelings both positive and negative | Self-esteem, feeling that you have power and can control and influence your experiences in the world |

Fig 1   Setting the context

After setting the context for the quality framework it is possible to identify specific issues that might be addressed by mental health promotion.

WHAT IS HEALTH?

Health is defined by the World Health Organization as a state of complete physical, mental and social well-being and not merely the absence of disease or injury. Good health is desired and valued in every society. It is the capacity, relative to potential and aspirations, for living fully in the social world (Tarlov, 1996). Mental health, as part of our overall health, is a resource which we need for everyday life which enables us to manage our lives successfully.

This concept of well-being can be separated into three key areas: needs, skills, and feelings and beliefs.

1. NEEDS

Complete well-being is underpinned by our basic needs being met. These needs are physical, mental and social, such as adequate food and shelter, survival, protection, security and social support; and freedom from pain, environmental hazards, unnecessary stress, and from any form of exploitation (Maslow, 1968). They underpin higher needs which affect our health such as affectionate relationships, the acceptance and significance given by others, membership of a group, approval, self respect and dignity, freedom and self fulfilment.
Our basic needs are affected by the provision of healthy structures in our community.

2. SKILLS

Complete well-being is underpinned by emotional skills. These skills include the ability to manage change, to recognise, acknowledge and communicate thoughts and feelings, both positive and negative. In addition, mental health involves the skills to make and maintain relationships, to cope with stress and/or to modify environments or relationships that cause stress. Mental health is about balance but it also includes abilities at the extremes e.g. the ability to be happy and sad, hopeful and despairing. Mental health promotion must not only focus on maintaining good mental health, but on developing the skills and resources required to survive mental health problems.
Our emotional skills affect, and are affected by, our experiences of the social world.

3. FEELINGS AND BELIEFS

Complete well-being is underpinned by our individual feelings and beliefs. These feelings include feeling that we have rights, feeling worthy, feeling that we have power and can control and influence our experiences in the world. It also involves an understanding and acceptance that psychological or emotional problems can and do occur in ourselves and others. In addition, mental health involves feeling positive about yourself and others, feeling glad, joyful and loving (SHEPS – 1996).
Our feelings and beliefs are affected by our experiences in early childhood and affect our ability to deal with the inner world.

WHAT IS MENTAL HEALTH?

Mental health is the emotional and spiritual resilience which enables us to enjoy life and to survive pain, suffering and disappointment. It is a positive sense of well-being and an underlying belief in our own and others' dignity and worth. Mental health is influenced by our genetic inheritance and by our experiences in three key areas:

1. HEALTHY STRUCTURES

Healthy social, economic and cultural structures provide a basic framework for developing and maintaining positive mental health.

Structural factors associated with an increased risk of mental health problems include unemployment, poor housing, inequality in income, discrimination, and limited opportunities to exercise choice or control. Education is a protective factor for mental health, notably pre-school education.

Examples of mental health promotion initiatives that aim to address healthy structures include:

- the establishment of a community development programme on the environment – increasing awareness and opportunities to participate among young people
- the creation of an anti-stigma campaign – increasing awareness about mental health, changing attitudes and increasing respect towards people experiencing mental health problems, reducing their distress, increasing integration and willingness to seek help
- the development of child/family health strategies – assessing the impact of current policies and practice on families, increasing family friendly policies in the workplace and the development of initiatives and services which support families
- the establishment of specific advocacy and interpretation initiatives – providing culturally appropriate advocates and interpreters, increasing awareness and understanding and ensuring access for all to services

2. CITIZENSHIP – SOCIAL WORLD

Social support, strong social networks, a sense of integration and social inclusion are key predictors for mental health. Loneliness and isolation increase the risk of suicide and major depression and also reduce people's ability to cope with stressful life events. A positive sense of belonging and participating in society and the recognition of diversity and mutual responsibility contribute to mental well-being.

Examples of mental health promotion initiatives that aim to enhance citizenship include:

- the establishment of mental health policies in the workplace – reducing the rate of absenteeism and increasing productivity through reducing organisational causes of stress, increasing opportunities for control, promoting awareness of mental health issues

- anti-bullying schemes – reducing the rate of physical and verbal abuse/ bullying within schools and increasing the self-esteem of pupils
- the development of a community safety policy - reducing the rates of crime and vandalism, increasing citizens' feelings of safety resulting in their increased use of public spaces

3. EMOTIONAL RESILIENCE – INNER WORLD

Emotional resilience relates to how people feel about themselves, the interpretation of events and people's ability to cope with stressful or adverse circumstances. Self-esteem, coping and life skills, and opportunities to make choices and exercise control over one's life increase emotional resilience and reduce mental distress. Emotional and physical neglect and deprivation in childhood inhibit the development of emotional resilience and greatly increase vulnerability to mental health problems.

Examples of mental health promotion initiatives that aim to increase emotional resilience include:

- parenting skills courses – increasing the confidence of young parents in dealing with their children, improving relationships between parents and children and parents and professionals
- life skills training – increasing appropriate services provided by primary health care teams increasing the coping strategies among older people, who may be particularly vulnerable
- the development of good childcare facilities – allowing parents to work and care for their children more effectively and children in turn to feel more cared for and therefore better able to learn and develop
- peer support programmes – for adolescents, to discourage alcohol and substance abuse
- training schemes for registered child minders, promoting understanding of the emotional needs of pre-school children

WHAT IS MENTAL HEALTH PROMOTION?

Health promotion is the process of enabling individuals and communities to increase control over the determinants of health and of disease and thereby to improve their health. (HEA, 1997)

Mental health promotion acknowledges the importance of psychological processes – how people think, feel, interpret and communicate – and the role the mind and the emotions play in our interactions and experiences at all levels.

Mental health promotion includes any activity which actively fosters good mental health, through increasing mental health-promoting factors, such as meaningful employment and decreasing those factors which damage or reduce good mental health, such as abuse and violence. Activities which promote mental health may also prevent mental illness, although mental health promotion may only occasionally be an integrated part of the provision of mental health services.

How does this help a commissioner needing to make investment priorities, or a provider wanting to bring together activities to make an impact on mental health for their client group, or health promotion agencies wanting to address good mental health in the community?

Current mental health strategies are frequently mental illness strategies. Mental health promotion needs to address those social and structural issues which affect mental health, as well as working at the individual level. Mental health promotion strategies should cover a range of activities and services delivered by a range of providers, to a range of people at different stages in their lives. They should cover the needs of individuals and communities, and incorporate different types of activities, from primary prevention to the delivery of services for people in the most extreme need. Mental health promotion includes services directed to a whole community, and not just to those people with existing mental health problems.

It is crucial to recognise that activities and interventions which promote mental health will be both health and non-health based. Good housing, having a job, access to services and buildings, activities which are directed to promoting health generally, such as family planning, sexual health and CHD programmes, as well as services directly targeted at the primary prevention of mental health problems are all able to deliver benefits for mental health.

It is also recognised that improving the physical environment, transport systems, housing, home and community infrastructure, work and the workplace, schools and health care settings will influence the mental health of the population. Therefore mental health promotion has a role in reducing the proportion of people who live below the poverty line, increasing the proportion of the population whose social environments provide adequate, appropriate social support and increasing the proportion of people who have access to appropriate, high quality social support services.

DEVELOPING A QUALITY FRAMEWORK FOR MENTAL HEALTH PROMOTION

The Quality Framework for Mental Health Promotion outlined in this document is one effective way of planning, delivering and evaluating mental health promotion.

Fig. 2 The quality cycle

The rest of this section looks at the constituent parts of the quality cycle, starting with needs assessment.

Effective mental health promotion sets out to meet the mental health needs of the individuals or communities which it aims to serve. These needs will be viewed in relation to national targets, local priorities, epidemiological evidence and consultation with the community. There are three underlying principles which underpin the needs assessment process, ensuring the effective delivery of mental health promotion interventions.

The need for mental health promotion is universal and of relevance to all of us

We all need mental health promotion – the positive promotion of good health through increasing personal and social strengths and the development of healthy communities. Mental health promotion is not only for those who are experiencing or who have experienced mental health problems, nor should it be solely aimed at individuals who are considered to be at risk. There is a role for interventions which target specific groups, due to budgetary constraints or to reduce inequalities. However, increasing healthy structures, a sense of citizenship and emotional resilience would benefit the mental health of the whole community.

Mental health promotion should reflect diverse needs and diverse approaches

Mental health is the result of many interacting factors and there is no single way to promote it. Communities are made up of a diverse range of people and although interventions cannot be tailored individually, they must consider diverse approaches to meet diverse needs. Issues such as race, class, gender, sexuality and differing religious beliefs should be considered, as they will affect the needs of the community, the effective delivery of an intervention, the accessibility and appropriateness of the programme and the way in which it is evaluated. Whether increasing healthy structures, a sense of citizenship or individual emotional resilience, diverse approaches should be developed.

The process used to promote mental health should itself be mental health promoting

Processes used to promote mental health should reflect best practice to ensure user involvement, meaningful consultation and participation, equal opportunities, recognition of diversity, open communication and accountability. Mental health promotion interventions need to address structural barriers to mental health, as well as focusing on individual responses. For example, a Mental Health in the Workplace policy will address organisational causes of stress, as well as individual stress management skills.

DETERMINANTS OF MENTAL HEALTH

The factors influencing mental health are a combination of genetic inheritance and socio-economic circumstances. Psychological variables, such as levels of self esteem, have an influence on the impact of socio-economic factors and the way in which individuals, families and communities respond to changing environments or life events, such as becoming a parent, retiring or being made redundant.

Which factors work to promote mental health, or to protect against ill health?
Which factors work to reduce mental health or create a greater vulnerability?

Identifying mental health promoting and mental health demoting factors will help to identify the individual mental health needs of the community, family or individual. They can also assist organisations to develop a culture and environment which promotes mental health at work.
Tables 1 and 2 give some examples of internal and external factors which promote (Table 1) and reduce (Table 2) opportunities for good mental health (see pp.14–15).

Table 1: Health promoting/protective factors

INTERNAL PROTECTIVE FACTORS	EXTERNAL PROTECTIVE FACTORS
	HEALTHY STRUCTURES ■ positive educational experiences, notably pre-school ■ safe and secure environment in which to live ■ supportive political infrastructure ■ live within time of peace (absence of conflict)
CITIZENSHIP ■ positive experience of early bonding ■ positive experience of attachment ■ ability to make, maintain and break relationships ■ communication skills ■ feeling of acceptance	**CITIZENSHIP** ■ societal or community validation of self ■ supportive social network ■ positive role models ■ employment ■ opportunuties to make choices, exercise control, develop skills
EMOTIONAL RESILIENCE ■ physical health ■ self-esteem/positive sense of self ■ ability to manage conflict ■ ability to learn ■ coping skills	**EMOTIONAL RESILIENCE** ■ basic needs met – food, warmth, shelter

Table 2: Health demoting/vulnerability factors

INTERNAL VULNERABILITY FACTORS	EXTERNAL VULNERABILITY FACTORS
	HEALTHY STRUCTURES ■ poverty ■ poor quality housing/physical environment ■ inequality ■ unemployment
CITIZENSHIP ■ poor quality of relationships ■ feeling of isolation ■ feeling of institutionalisation ■ experience of dissonance, conflict, or alienation	**CITIZENSHIP** ■ cultural conflict – experience of alienation ■ discrimination ■ stigma ■ lack of autonomy ■ the negative experience of peer pressure ■ unemployment
EMOTIONAL RESILIENCE ■ congenital illness, infirmity or disability ■ lack of self-esteem and social status ■ feeling of helplessness ■ problems with sexuality or sexual orientation	**EMOTIONAL RESILIENCE** ■ needs not being met – hunger, cold, homelessness/poor housing conditions etc ■ experience of separation and loss ■ experience of abuse or violence ■ substance misuse ■ family history of psychiatric disorder

This chapter aims to outline the effectiveness of mental health promotion activities. A more detailed review of the literature summarised in this chapter is included in Appendix 1. Much of the work on effectiveness in mental health promotion has not been widely disseminated and there are few examples based on UK initiatives. In particular, interventions involving social and environmental change are poorly represented, as there has been little research in this area.

Another important consideration is the difference between preventing mental illness and promoting mental health. Much of the good research evidence has been directed towards the prevention of mental health problems. However, it is generally accepted that interventions which prevent mental disorders also promote mental health and interventions that promote mental health also prevent mental disorders. Similarly, the links between physical and mental health suggest that a single commissioning strategy should emphasise the mental health impact of all health promotion activity.

Mental health promotion interventions can be effective. Given the fact that mental health is linked to a wide range of influences it is not surprising that the best interventions focus upon more than one factor. A meta study by Bosma and Hosman (1990), for example, identified the following elements as crucial to a successful multi-component approach directed towards influencing a combination of risk or protective factors:

- it should involve relevant parts of the social network of the target group such as parents, teachers or family

- it should intervene at a range of different times rather than once only

- it should use a combination of intervention methods (e.g. developing social support and coping skills).

There is also a developing body of interest and information, particularly stemming from user interest, in alternative and complementary approaches to the management of mental illness and to mental health promotion. The Mental Health Foundation's report *Knowing our own minds* (1997) outlines a strong perspective on this.

This chapter summarises the evidence collated by Tilford *et al.* (1997) and by Hodgson and Abassi (1995) for the Health Education Authority and for Health Promotion Wales respectively. Therefore, rather than being an exhaustive list of possibilities it is a summary of what we know to date.

SOME CHARACTERISTICS OF PEOPLE AT HIGH RISK OF DEVELOPING MENTAL HEALTH PROBLEMS

Outlined below is a list of at risk groups where specific interventions have been successful in promoting mental health.

Children

- exhibiting behavioural difficulties
- experiencing bereavement
- experiencing parental separation or divorce
- living in poverty

Adults

- at risk of experiencing depression in pregnancy
- experiencing bereavement
- experiencing separation or divorce
- long term carers of people who are highly dependent
- unemployed

SUMMARY OF EFFECTIVE INTERVENTIONS

Broadly similar approaches across the spectrum of mental health promotion have been found to be effective. These include:

- promoting good social relationships, for example, through social skills and assertiveness training, as well as communication and relationship skills

- developing effective coping skills, such as problem solving skills, cognitive skills and parenting skills

- providing social support and making social changes: examples include changing school attitudes regarding bullying, home visits from health workers to support new parents, supporting bereaved families, supporting widows and carers

- the evidence also suggests that mass media campaigns supported by community activities can have a measurable impact on knowledge, attitudes and behavioural intentions.

Infants and pre-school children

■ Home-based intervention to high risk families/children

These programmes provide social support while focusing on parent-child interactions. They can result in better family management, fewer developmental delays and behaviour problems.

■ Pre-school education programmes

These programmes contribute to reducing inequality and conduct disorders.

School-age children

■ Effective school-based programmes

There are a number of effective school based programmes which focus upon improving social and cognitive competence as well as reducing substance misuse and aggressive behaviour for a particular age group.

■ School-based programmes for children exhibiting behavioural problems

These programmes focus mainly on social relationships, approval for good behaviour and some parental involvement. They can reduce aggressive behaviour, improve school performance, and reduce delinquent behaviour.

■ Programmes for children experiencing bereavement or parental separation or divorce

These programmes focus on dealing with feelings of loss, conflict and anger and can result in a reduction of mental health problems among the target group.

Adult and elderly populations

■ Programmes for adults experiencing separation and divorce

As with programmes directed at children, these initiatives can reduce psychiatric symptoms even in the longer term.

■ Programmes for women who have experienced a caesarean delivery

Caesarean deliveries have been shown to lead to increased rates of post-natal depression. A relatively brief intervention can reduce psychological problems, reduce medication and enhance attachment between parents and baby.

■ Home visiting programmes

Programmes which focus upon parenting skills and the prevention of psychological problems in children also result in better mental health outcomes for mothers.

- Programmes for carers

  Programmes for those who care for people who are elderly, disabled or mentally ill which aim to increase social support networks, increase social interaction and decrease isolation can help to reduce the level of stress that carers experience and reduce the incidence of abuse of older people.

- Programmes for the unemployed

  These programmes aim to enhance confidence, increase motivation and reduce the negative feelings related to unemployment and can result in unemployed people becoming more able to deal with feelings of helplessness and depression and their chances of finding a job can also be increased. Less negative social attitudes to unemployment increase people's ability to cope.

- Programmes for newly widowed women

  These programmes aim to increase social support and information and they can lead to individuals increasing their uptake of new activities and social relationships as well as reducing levels of depression.

People experiencing either a severe or a less disabling mental health or behavioural problem

- Programmes advocating or providing aerobic exercise, cognitive-behavioural interventions and social support

  These programmes can reduce moderate levels of depression.

- Programmes focusing on motivation to change

  These programmes can ameliorate some alcohol-related problems through brief interventions.

- Programmes focusing on coping skills, social skills and community involvement

  These programmes can reduce more severe alcohol-related problems.

- Family interventions for schizophrenia

  These programmes have been shown to be effective in preventing relapse and subsequent hospital admissions.

STRATEGIC PLANNING

A strategic framework for mental health promotion helps to ensure the appropriate allocation of budgets and joint planning across professional and agency boundaries. This framework approach is underpinned by needs assessment of the community and drawing on the research effectiveness review to identify the most appropriate interventions.

The framework will plot or map mental health promotion activity, to identify gaps, agree priorities/targets and avoid duplication. The three dimensions for the framework are:

level of action:
- international
- national
- regional
- local community
- family
- individual

stage of life:
- infancy
- childhood
- adolescence
- early adulthood
- mid life
- old age

and
settings for action:
- home
- school
- workplace
- community
- provider service
- media

The framework can assist in identifying areas of responsibility, highlighting services with untapped mental health promotion potential or opportunities for multi-agency strategies e.g. to improve media coverage of mental health issues within a region.

Considering the type of activity – is it education? campaigning? advocacy? development of self help groups? better workplace environments? good respite care for carers? – enables a review of the whole set of approaches used to promote the mental health of the community.

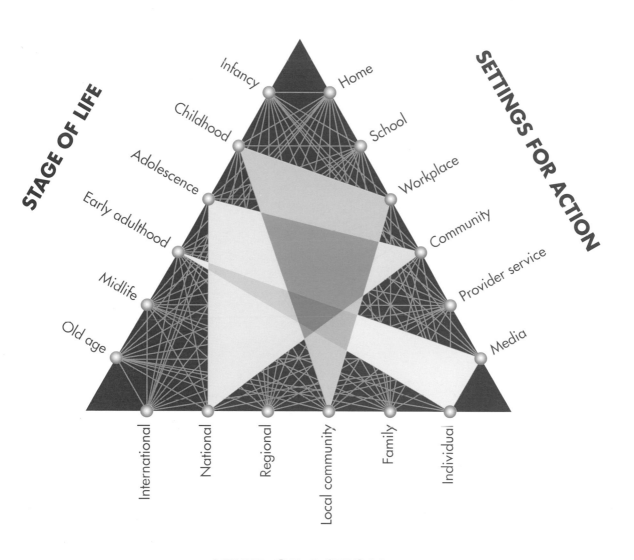

STAGE OF LIFE

Infancy
Childhood
Adolescence
Early adulthood
Midlife
Old age

SETTINGS FOR ACTION

Home
School
Workplace
Community
Provider service
Media

International
National
Regional
Local community
Family
Individual

LEVEL OF ACTION

Fig. 3 A 'map' for mental health promotion

Indicators provide a means to measure the achievements of mental health promotion. Measuring the success of mental health promotion is relatively new and most of us are unsure of how precisely to proceed, although there is a developing body of evidence to guide us. If the profile of mental health promotion is to be raised, and investment of resources in the area increased, it is crucial to demonstrate that approaches and interventions are effective, evidence based, and able to offer value for money.

WHAT ARE INDICATORS?

Glover and Kamis-Gould (1996) write that 'performance indicators are operationally defined, indirect measures of selected aspects of a system which give some indication of how far it conforms with its intended purpose'.

In the field of health promotion, there has grown up a convention of four types of indicator to evaluate performance:

- **input** is the specific resources that go into an initiative: the staffing and material resources
- **process** is what actually happens during the initiative: what the people involved do and what use the materials are put to
- **impact** refers to the consequences that can be attributed to the process activity: personal changes of all sorts, activity of other people, changes in processes and procedures, provision of facilities, environmental change, organisational change
- **outcome** relates back to the goal of the activity – the end product

Indicators can be direct measures within a project or indirect measures which point to whether the impact of an intervention is on the way to effecting wider, more sustained and more general mental health outcomes.

Indicators should be
- specific
- measurable
- reliable
- valid
- realistic
- practical
- cost effective
- evidence based
- ethical

Indicators need to be embedded in the strategies for developing mental health promotion within the community. The tools for measuring the indicators should be linked to the needs of the community and consistent with the goals of the activity.

Input indicators will involve the time and resources required to carry out the work. Examples might include identifying goals, funds and research to support the approach to be taken.

Process indicators are commonly used indicators for mental health promotion. Examples might be number of sessions of a group held, evidence of multi-disciplinary planning, consultation with the community and target groups/users, the activity going ahead, getting funding, evaluation. Process indicators concentrate on the way in which the process of mental health promotion is carried out, from the initial planning through to the evaluation.

Impact indicators might be changes in knowledge and skills, greater sense of confidence, reduction of bullying in schools, higher rates of social interaction, more people voting, less truancy, more neighbourhood watch schemes.

Outcome indicators have been notoriously difficult to measure, since outcomes are the cumulative result of a range of interventions and activities. In programmes with a clear set of parameters and a clear linear progression, outcomes will relate directly to the aims and objectives of the work. However, because of the multi-factorial and multi-disciplinary nature of mental health promotion, the outcomes may be more difficult to link back to specific interventions.

EXAMPLES OF INDICATORS

Indicators which might reflect the outcomes could include:
For healthy structures
- user involvement
- equal opportunities
- reduction in inequalities
- healthy public policy

For citizenship
- awareness and respect of self and others
- effective communication skills
- sense of belonging
- increased social support/networks

For emotional resilience
- effective coping skills and strategies
- self-esteem
- assertiveness

Input indicators:

- the authority/organisation has a strategy for mental health promotion, which includes a clear financial commitment and commissioning intentions
- the strategy includes a range of mental health promotion activities, to cover different approaches undertaken at different levels, at different stages in people's lives and in different health promotion settings

Process indicators:

- mental health promotion is jointly commissioned
- mental health promotion is audited
- mental health impact statements are included in all contracts
- changes in service activity

Impact indicators:

- commissioning plans increasingly reflect mental health promotion
- monitoring indicates changes in the desired direction – increase in complaints made, reduction in bullying problems in schools, healthy public policies, all policies include mental health impact statements, greater impact of services
- positive changes identified in scores on General Health Questionnaire

Outcome indicators:

- needs assessment reflects better health
- reduction in suicide rates

MENTAL HEALTH PROMOTION AUDIT

Indicators are the key 'markers' for auditing or assessing the effectiveness and progress of your activity. In this document we are using the term audit to relate to the whole process of review, rather than concentrating solely on for example, an audit of the mental health needs of a community or an audit of service delivery.

A mental health promotion audit would, therefore, largely follow the mental health promotion quality framework model to:

- assess the mental health needs of a community
- identify the factors which either promote or demote the mental health of the community
- consider the effectiveness of initiatives currently being undertaken or planned
- map the current policies, initiatives and services which have an impact on the mental health of the community
- plan and deliver more mental health promotion through inter-disciplinary and multi-agency working across all sectors and at all levels
- evaluate the mental health impact of current initiatives.

The outcomes of mental health promotion activity may take some time to be fully realised, the importance of process and impact indicators as measures of 'progress in the right direction' is high. Each input, process and impact indicator builds into the final cumulative outcome.

MENTAL HEALTH IMPACT

Mental health promotion audit provides a framework for assessing the mental health impact of policy and practice at all levels and across all sectors. It is a model which has been successfully used in areas like equal opportunities and sustainable development. By considering the mental health implications of policy and practice, awareness of mental health and mental health promotion will be raised and the substantial social and economic costs of mental distress will be reduced.

Mental health impact is relevant to a very diverse range of agencies across all sectors:

- in the workplace, it provides a framework for assessing how management and organisational factors impact on mental health and for including issues like stress within health and safety policies
- in local authorities, it provides an opportunity to integrate mental health into the planning cycle, notably in areas like housing, leisure, pre-school education and transport.
- it is integral to community development initiatives in tackling fundamental challenges including consultation, participation, empowerment and accountability
- for service providers it has potential in areas including user involvement, restoring public confidence and needs assessment.

Mental health impact statements could, therefore, be built into the planning and review cycles of local authorities, health authorities and Government departments.

PLANNING THE ACTIVITY – Checklist

1. What are your goals?
   What needs are you addressing?
   What resources are available?
   How does your work build on what you already know?
   How complimentary is the work in relation to other elements of health promotion?
   What empirical backing is already available and how relevant is it?
   What level of support is there from the available theory?

2. Who is your target group?
   What proportion of the whole population is covered?
   How cumulative is the impact of the intervention likely to be in the future?
   How might the impact of the work 'ripple out' into the wider population?

3. What is your consultation and involvement strategy?
   What assets and strengths exist in the consultation group?
   How will you involve the target groups/users?
   What factors are likely to affect or diminish the effect of the work?

4a. How will this work be implemented?
   Has needs assessment identified strengths as well as weaknesses ?
   Have you allowed adequate time for each stage?
   Does the team 'own' the work?
   Have you planned in target group/user involvement at each stage including the choice of indicators?

4b. Have you planned/carried out a pilot?

5. What success criteria have you established for your evaluation?
   What indicators have you set?
   How do your indicators relate to your key goals?

6. How will you audit your work?
   How will the work be sustained?

7. What are the implications for further action?
   How sustainable is the impact of the work likely to be?

8. How will the dissemination of findings or results happen?

GOOD PRACTICE – Checklist

1   What are the professional supervision/management arrangements?

2   What is the training plan for staff ?

3   How does the work link with your business plan and corporate policies, e.g. equal opportunities?

TARGET GROUP/USER INVOLVEMENT – Process Checklist

1 How have you defined the criteria for involvement ?

2 How have you defined methods to allow people to become involved?

3 What are your expectations of target group representatives/users? How have you made them known?

4 How appropriate is the environment you are using ?

5 How do you know how many representatives/users to involve?

6 Is there equality, belonging and diversity among the group? How do you know?

7 What range of options for representative/user involvement have you explored? How will you explore them and come to a decision?

8 How will you identify the strengths to promote, not just deficits to address?

9 How will target group/user involvement be facilitated?

10 How will target group/user involvement be supported?

11 How have you addressed equality?

12 How does the membership reflect the goals of the work?

TARGET GROUP/USER INVOLVEMENT – Process Indicators

1   Expectations of representatives/user involvement and contribution are clearly stated

2   Drop out rate is low/zero

3   Number of individuals leaving the scheme/project is low

4   Numbers involved and attending each individual activity are high

5   Materials have been tested with the target groups/users of the resource

6   Satisfaction of target groups/users with process and project content - measures

7   Target groups'/users' voice fairly reflected in all written outputs

HEALTHY STRUCTURES
Example 1

KEY GOAL	LEVEL	LIFESTAGE	SETTING
	international	infancy	home
	national	childhood	school
	regional		workplace
resilience		adolescence	
	local community	early adulthood	community
citizenship	family	mid life	health service
healthy structures	individual	old age	media

LEVEL	Local community – local authority boundary
LIFESTAGE	Young people (11-16 years)
SETTING	Community-wide
PROJECT	Environmental awareness – community development
AIMS	To increase environmental/community awareness among young people
OBJECTIVES	To identify young people who would benefit from awareness raising
	To improve the target group's understanding and respect for the local environment
	To increase the number of young people involved in the development of the community
MONITORING	Project to run over two years, co-ordinated by the local authority
	Project co-ordinator to report to relevant links within the authority quarterly (elected representatives bi-annually)
	Project operation team to meet bi-weekly to discuss operational issues
	Each individual scheme will produce a final report which will be presented at a local Agenda 21 conference

INDICATORS

Input   Project co-ordinator recruited (internal position within the authority)
Identification of a number of secondary schools and youth organisations
and clubs interested in being involved in the programme

Process   Target group/user consultation forum established
Development of resources for youth leaders, raising issues around
ownership of your community and environmental awareness
Project co-ordinator presents resources to each agency involved

Impact   Increased time spent in schools concerning environmental and
community issues
Increase in the number of small projects run by youth groups and
agencies, funded by the local authority relating to the environment and
community
Increased time spent in youth agencies developing work and projects on
environmental and community issues
Self reported increased feelings of community identification

Outcomes   Increase in the 'sense of community'
Reduction in vandalism
Increase in the number of young voters, both for national and local
elections

HEALTHY STRUCTURES
Example 2

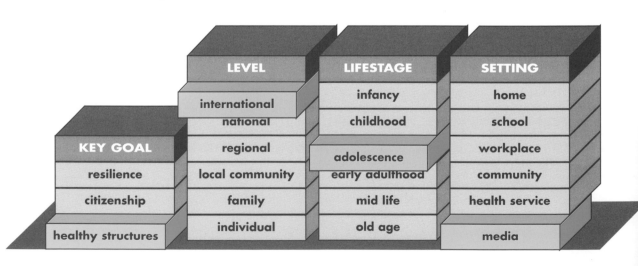

LEVEL	International
LIFESTAGE	General with particular relevance for adolescents
SETTING	Media
PROJECT	Anti-sigma international campaign
AIMS	To reduce the stigma within society towards people who have experienced mental health problems

OBJECTIVES
To run development days for journalists to raise their awareness of mental health issues
To decrease the stigmatising language used by the international media
To increase more accurate reporting of events involving an individual who has experienced a mental health problem

MONITORING
Project to run over three years, co-ordinated by an International health agency aiming to promote global mental health into the next millennium
Annual reports on the development in each country will be submitted to the funder
Quarterly monitoring meetings of heads of regions will review progress made to date

INDICATORS

Input
Identify and recruit representatives in specific countries
International co-ordinator elected

Process
Establishment of a global target group/user forum and individual national target group/user forums
Launch event held – high profile event to raise awareness of the issues
Terms of reference for consultation forum developed and implemented
Development days held and evaluated (run by adolescents, users and health professionals)

Impact
Number of journalists attending development days
How useful the journalists considered the development days to be
Shifts in attitude among journalists

Outcomes
Increased recognition among adolescents of what is stigmatising language
Decrease in the use of stigmatising words within the written press
Increase in positive imagery throughout the media

HEALTHY STRUCTURES – SOCIAL LEVEL
Example 3

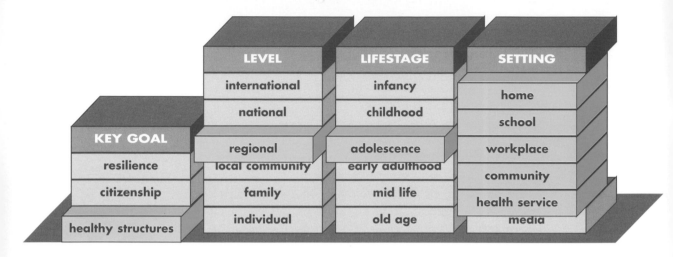

LEVEL	LIFESTAGE	SETTING
international	infancy	home
national	childhood	school
regional	adolescence	workplace
local community	early adulthood	community
family	mid life	health service
individual	old age	media

KEY GOAL
- resilience
- citizenship
- healthy structures

LEVEL	Regional
LIFESTAGE	Young people
SETTING	Multi-agency
PROJECT	Child/family health strategy
AIMS	To develop mental health promoting child/family welfare services through the development of a 'family friendly' policy, applicable throughout the region
OBJECTIVES	To establish a strategy forum of relevant individuals from key agencies To agree a 'family friendly' policy for the region and to ensure its implementation To increase the uptake of relevant services through an increased sense of community and recognition of the importance of the family as a social structure
MONITORING	Project to run indefinitely, co-ordination post within the health authority Progress reports will be submitted to the strategy forum bi-annually Individual representatives will submit annual reports to their relevant organisations
INDICATORS Input	Identify key agencies, including health, social, welfare agencies, voluntary and statutory

              Gain organisational commitment from all the key agencies
              Review the literature on strategic approaches to child/family policy
              implementation and the mental health impacts

Process   Recruit relevant individuals to represent their organisations
              Establishment of strategy forum through recruitment of relevant
              representatives
              Establishment of a parent/carer forum to inform the work of strategy
              group

Impact   Increased awareness in key agencies of the importance of a strategic
              approach to the mental health impact of child/family welfare
              Increased links between key agencies, both commissioning and
              providing

Outcomes Increased number of agencies working towards a 'family friendly' policy
              in the provision of child/family welfare
              Increased provision of appropriate client centred services and schemes
              Increased client uptake and satisfaction

CITIZENSHIP
Example 1

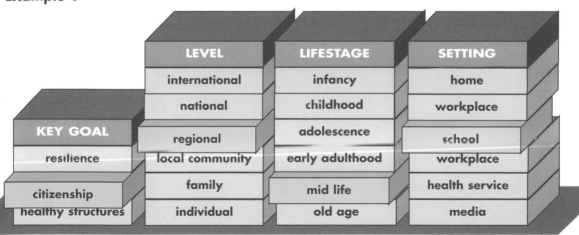

KEY GOAL	LEVEL	LIFESTAGE	SETTING
	international	infancy	home
	national	childhood	workplace
resilience	regional	adolescence	school
	local community	early adulthood	workplace
citizenship	family	mid life	health service
healthy structures	individual	old age	media

LEVEL   Regional
LIFESTAGE Working adult population
SETTING   Workplace
PROJECT   Mentally healthy workplaces
AIMS   To improve mental health awareness in the workplace

OBJECTIVES	To produce a resource pack for individual employers To develop mental health promotion policies among individual employers for specific workplaces To increase the awareness among employers and employees of issues affecting mental health
MONITORING	Project to run over one year, co-ordinated by a local group of occupational nurses Monthly meetings for nurses involved and consultants employed to advise on workplace policies Bi-monthly meetings for the project workers and the employers involved Quarterly meetings with project workers and staff representatives of individual workplaces
INDICATORS **Input**	Identify individual employers willing to be involved with the programme Review the literature on effective mental health promotion workplace programmes Identify resources and establish brief for the programme
Process	Consultation on the issues affecting the mental health of employees Establishment of a target group/user forum Materials developed and disseminated
Impact	Uptake of materials by employers Number of employers who have developed mental health policies within their workplaces Number of discussions between management and individual employees about mental health issues
Outcome	Cultural change within the organisations Increased productivity due to the development of a mentally healthy workforce Reduction in the number of disciplinary issues brought before managers Reduction of absenteeism, more honesty in completing absence forms

CITIZENSHIP
Example 2

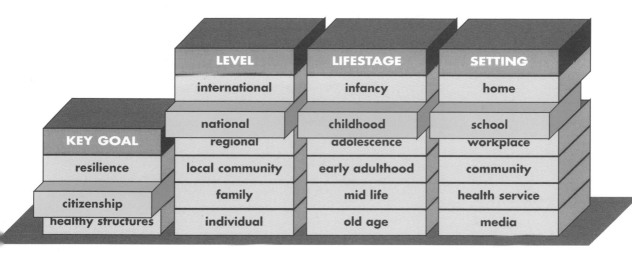

LEVEL	National
LIFESTAGE	Children (7–11 years)
SETTING	School
PROJECT	Anti-bullying schemes within primary schools
AIMS	To reduce the impact of bullying in primary schools in England

OBJECTIVES To develop anti-bullying strategies in all primary schools
To increase awareness of bullying among primary school teachers
To improve the coping strategies of pupils, ensuring a self-policing policy
for children

MONITORING Project to run over five years, co-ordinated by a national agency with a
brief to develop the rights of children
Individual school reports submitted annually
Annual meetings of pupils' forum
Annual meetings of teachers' forum

INDICATORS
Input Review the international literature on mental health promotion in schools
and anti-bullying campaigns
Links made with individuals responsible for national curriculum
integration and lesson planning

Process   Consultation forums established and timetabled
Consultation process implemented - relevant teacher and pupil
representatives elected
Classes relating to bullying timetabled in to the schools' yearplans
Establishment of a target group/user forum

Impact   Increased awareness among teachers of 'signs' of bullying
Increase in the class time spent discussing social issues, including
bullying
Increase in the number of bullying incidences reported, numbers of
incidences fall gradually over the length of the programme

Outcomes   Reduction in the number of bullying incidences
Reduction in visits to the school nurse with bullying related injuries
Reduction in truancy figures

CITIZENSHIP - SOCIAL LEVEL
Example 3

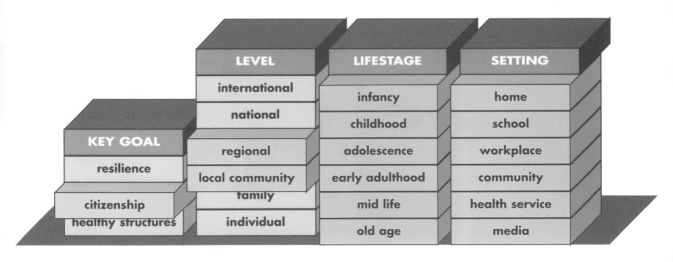

LEVEL   City
LIFESTAGE   All stages
SETTING   Multi-agency
PROJECT   Community safety policy
AIMS   To increase the safety and the perception of safety among the general
public within the city's open spaces

OBJECTIVES To establish a strategy forum of relevant individuals from key agencies
To agree a community safety policy for the region and to ensure its implementation
To increase the numbers of people accessing the city's open spaces

MONITORING Project to run indefinitely, co-ordination post within the local authority
Progress reports will be submitted to the local authority bi-annually
Individual representatives will submit annual reports to their relevant organisations

INDICATORS

Input Identify key agencies, including health, social, the police, leaders of neighbourhood watch schemes and voluntary agencies such as Victim Support and Rape Crisis Centre
Gain organisational commitment and resources to take the work forward
Review the literature on strategic approaches to community safety policy implementation and the mental health impacts

Process Recruit relevant individuals to represent their organisations
Establishment of strategy forum through recruitment of relevant representatives
Establishment of a target group/user forum to inform the work of strategy group

Impact Successful completion of a number of public events where the new community safety policy and the implications of its implementation were presented to the public
Increased profile and visibility for community workers and police
Increased numbers of neighbourhood watch schemes established

Outcomes Decreased number of crimes committed in open spaces
Decreased incidence of vandalism and damage to public property in open spaces
Increased number of individuals accessing the city's open spaces
Increased number of new uses for the city's open spaces

EMOTIONAL RESILIENCE
Example 1

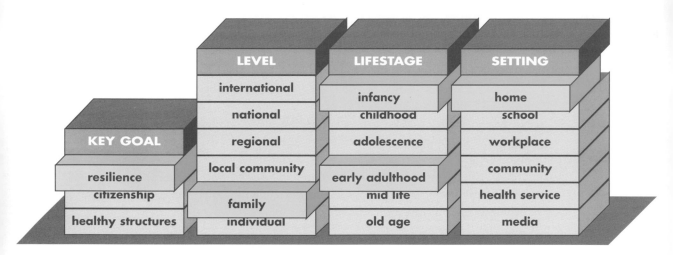

LEVEL	Family
LIFESTAGE	Young adults (16–24 years) and infants
SETTING	Home
PROJECT	Parenting skills for first time parents
AIMS	To help young parents to develop parenting skills promoting the mental health of themselves and their children
OBJECTIVES	To identify and prioritise young parents who would benefit from parenting skills training To collate relevant information on bonding and the development of meaningful relationships To arrange practical support, particularly for lone parents
MONITORING	Project to run until 100 parents have gained training, co-ordinated by health visitors Project co-ordinator meeting with individual health visitors weekly Individual brief precis reports on each individual case, submitted for review by project co-ordinator Full project meetings on a monthly basis where summary reports are discussed by the project team

INDICATORS

Input   Identify resources and establish project brief
Recruit a project co-ordinator
Literature review on bonding and attachment and development of practical guidance

Process   Recruitment and briefing of health visitors
Establishment of a target group/user forum for consultation
Health visitor training undertaken and evaluated

Impact   Shifts in attitude among health visitors
Increased health visitors time spent with young parents
Improved levels of job satisfaction among health visitors

Outcomes   Improved parenting skills among young parents
Increased awareness among young parents of the relevance of bonding and early relationships
Improved relationships between health visitors and clients

EMOTIONAL RESILIENCE
Example 2

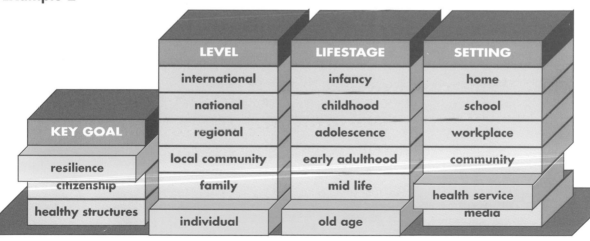

LEVEL   Individual
LIFESTAGE   Older people
SETTING   Health service – primary care
PROJECT   Life skills training for older people
AIMS   To improve the coping strategies of older people, particularly around times of bereavement

OBJECTIVES   To produce a resource pack for local primary care surgeries on the impacts of bereavement among older people and proven positive coping strategies to promote mental health, linked with depression in the elderly and the Defeat Depression Campaign
To produce resources for older people, to be given by the GPs to those currently experiencing a bereavement
To produce resources for older people, around general mental health promotion, to be given by the GPs in regular healthcheck visits

MONITORING   Project to run over three years, co-ordinated by the local health promotion unit
Annual reports required by commissioners outlining the development and uptake of resources, as well as the applicability to target audiences and the use made of information gained

INDICATORS

Input   GP surgeries identified to be involved in the programme
Individuals within each identified practice recruited to take responsibility for the programme
Identify resources and establish brief for the programme

Process   Consultation of the development of materials – meetings held
Establishment of target group/user forum for consultation
Materials developed and disseminated

Impact   Uptake of materials within GP surgeries
Increase in members of the surgery aware of the resource
Increase in number of patients requesting resources

Outcome   Improved awareness among primary care professionals of coping strategies among older people
Improved coping strategies among older people
Reduced GP consultations among older people following a bereavement

EMOTIONAL RESILIENCE – SOCIAL LEVEL
Example 3

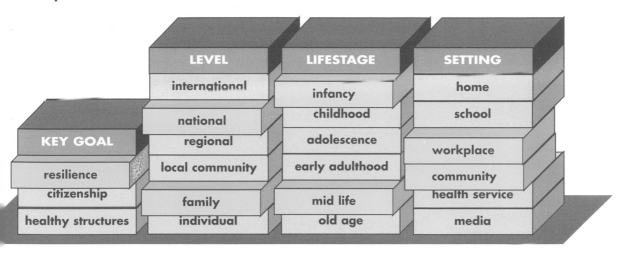

LEVEL	LIFESTAGE	SETTING
international	infancy	home
national	childhood	school
regional	adolescence	workplace
local community	early adulthood	community
family	mid life	health service
individual	old age	media

KEY GOAL: resilience, citizenship, healthy structures

LEVEL	Family and national
LIFESTAGE	Mid-life and infancy
SETTING	Workplace and community
PROJECT	Childcare provision strategy
AIMS	To develop good quality childcare provision promoting the mental health of working parents and their children
OBJECTIVES	To establish a strategy forum of relevant individuals from key agencies To agree a strategy and methods of implementation and review To increase awareness among employers of the need for quality childcare provision To increase the uptake of employer based childcare provision
MONITORING	Project to run indefinitely, co-ordinated by local authorities Project co-ordinator meeting with all regional childcare services Monthly monitoring reports required by employers involved within the scheme Annual reports required by local authorities, quantitative and qualitative data
INDICATORS **Input**	Identify resources and establish a project brief Identify key agencies, including trade unions, employers associations, childcare services, welfare agencies – voluntary and statutory

Review the literature on childcare provision and mental health promotion within the workplace and the family

Process

Establishment of strategy forum through recruitment of relevant representatives

Consultation of the development of minimum standards and accessibility

Establishment of parent/employer forum for consultation

Impact

Uptake of childcare provision

Increase in the appropriateness and accessibility of childcare provision within individual workplaces

Self reported increased feelings of being valued as a member of a workforce and as a parent

Outcome

Improved relationships between parent and child and parent and employer

Reduction in absenteeism, due to failing childcare provision

Decrease in disruptive behaviour among children

SELECTED REFERENCES – EFFECTIVENESS

This section aims to provide a reading list of relevant references but also to elaborate on the summary of findings described in Section Six through the provision of a very brief abstract of each. All these articles are based on findings from randomised control trials. Many of the outcomes however relate to variables which are known to be risk factors for mental health problems rather than positive factors for mental health (e.g. improved school performance or alcohol misuse) - although lessons for mental health promotion can be learnt.

Programmes directed at pre-school children

1. Field T.M, Widmayer, S.M., Stiner, S. & Ignatoff, E. (1980). Teenage, lower-class black mothers and their preterm infants: An intervention and developmental follow-up. *Child Development* **51**: 426–436.
A bi-weekly, home based, parental training intervention was provided for teenage mothers with preterm infants. The programme was designed to educate mothers on developmental milestones and child rearing practices, teach the mothers exercises and age appropriate stimulation to facilitate development of their infants, and to facilitate mother-infant interactions in the interest of developing communication skills and fostering mother-infant relationships. Positive outcome measures were shown on variables such as the baby's development at 8 months and mother's child rearing attitudes at 4 months.

2. Strayhorn, J.M. & Weidman, C.S. (1991). Follow-up one year after parent-child interaction training: Effects on behaviour of pre-school children. *Journal of American Academy of Child and Adolescent Psychiatry* **30**: 138–143.
The parent training intervention included group training, involving instruction and role playing practice. The individual sessions involved modeling and practice in conducting sessions of conversation, story reading and dramatic play with the child. At one year follow-up teacher ratings of children's behaviour in the intervention group showed significantly greater improvements. These ratings were a composite of hostility, anxiety and hyperactivity.

3. Field, T.M., Schanberg, S.M., Scafidi, F., Bauer, C.R., Vega-Lahr, N., Garcia, R., Nystrom, J. & Kuhn, C. (1986). Tactile/kinesthetic stimulation effects on preterm neonates. *Paediatrics* **77**: 654–659.
Infants in the intervention group received tactile/kinesthetic stimulation for three 15 minute periods at the beginning of three consecutive hours for ten weekdays. The 15 minute stimulation sessions consisted of three 5 minute phases. Tactile stimulation (gentle stroking of the baby's body and limbs) was given during the first and third phases, and kinesthetic stimulation (passive flexion/extension movements of the limbs) was given during the middle phase. The intervention group averaged a 47 per cent greater weight gain per day, were more active and alert and finally, their hospital stay was six days shorter.

4. Johnson, D.L. (1990). The Houston Parent-Child Development Centre Project: Disseminating a viable program for enhancing at-risk families. *Prevention in Human Sciences* **7**: 89–108.
Mothers with a young child were visited in their own homes by 'paraprofessional in-home educators' who provided 25 one and a half hour lessons. The topics covered included awareness of development, encouraging language development, encouraging curiosity and making use of inexpensive toys to promote cognitive development. In the second year of the intervention mothers and their children attended a special centre for four mornings a week where they were taught to manage problem behaviours and home management. At follow-up teacher ratings indicate a reduction of obstinate, disruptive and aggressive behaviour.

5. Shure, M.B. & Spivack, G. (1982). Interpersonal problem-solving in young children: A cognitive approach to prevention. *American Journal of Community Psychology* **10**: 341–351.
The intervention consisted of daily 20 minute sessions over a period of 8 weeks. Nursery aged children were taught skills to help them think about solutions and consequences relevant to hypothetical interpersonal problems. Pictures, puppets and simple role-playing techniques were used to facilitate these processes. A significant amount of the behaviour gains observed seemed to be due to the children acquiring new cognitive skills. Identified aberrant behaviours in the intervention group were less likely to persist to the end of kindergarten.

6. Olds, D.L., Henderson, C., Tatelbaum, R., Chamberlin, R. (1986). Preventing child abuse and neglect: A randomised trial of nurse home visitation. *Paediatrics* **78**: 65–78.
An intensive home visiting programme for high risk primipara mothers was implemented by Community Nurses. The intervention aimed to: educate parents on child development; encourage good parenting skills; enhance informal support to the mother and family; and facilitate links with appropriate outside agencies. Positive outcomes were associated with the intervention group. The incidence of abuse and neglect remained relatively low, even in those groups at higher risk and babies had higher developmental quotients at 12 months and 24 months than those in the control group.

7. Schweinhart, L.J., Weikart, D.P., & Larner, M.B. (1986). A report on the High/Scope pre-school curriculum comparison study: consequences of three pre-school curriculum models through age 15. *Early Childhood Quarterly* **1**: 15-45.
The programme is a cognitively orientated pre-school curriculum aimed at 3 year old children with IQ scores between 60-90. It was designed to teach children at risk of school failure the skills needed to meet the demands of schooling. The programme consisted of two components: classroom sessions of 2½ hours for 5 days a week as well as educational home visits in which a teacher visited each mother and child at home for 90 minute sessions every two weeks. Mothers were encouraged to assist the children in a range of learning activities. There were positive outcome measures on variables such as IQ and social behaviour through to age ten. At the age of 15 years self reports showed that children in the programme group were less likely to engage in delinquent acts.

8. Ramey, C.T. & Smith, B.J. (1976). Assessing the intellectual consequences of early intervention with high-risk infants. *American Journal of Mental Deficiency* **81**(4): 318-324.
The intervention was designed to prevent mental developmental delay by increasing family support, nutritional supplements and complete medical care. Children (between 6 and 12 weeks of age) attended an educational day-care centre. The curriculum was individually prescribed to encourage development in perception, cognition, language, social and motor development. Positive trends were shown on measurable intellectual performance in the first eighteen

months of life for infants in the programme group.

9. Tadmor, C.S., Brandes, J.M. & Hofman, J.E. (1988). Preventive Intervention for a caesarean birth population. *Journal of Preventive Psychiatry* **3**(4): 343-364.
The programme aimed to reduce mental health problems in women who had delivered infants by caesarean birth. This was achieved by: increasing natural and organised support systems, giving mothers clear and concise information, sharing the decision making process and developing task orientated activity to enhance emotional, cognitive and behavioural control.

Programmes directed at school age children

10. Caplan, M., Weissber, P.R., Grober, J.S., Sivo, P.J., Grady, K. & Jacoby, C. (1992). Social competence promotion with inner-city and suburban young adolescents: Effects on social adjustment and alcohol use. *Journal of Consulting and Clinical Psychology* **60**(1): 56–63.
The intervention is a social competence programme which incorporates general strategies as well as specific skills targeted at substance use prevention in young adolescents. The programme was presented in six classes during two 59 minute class periods per week over a fifteen week period. Participants were taught by didactic instruction, class discussion, videotapes, diaries, role playing, work sheets and home work assignments. Positive outcome measures on variables such as coping skills, social and emotional adjustment and the use of alcohol and drugs were shown at follow up.

11. Lochman, J.E. (1995). Screening of child behaviour problems for prevention programmes at school entry. *Journal of Consulting and Clinical Psychology* **63**(4): 549–559.
This is a school and family based fast track programme. It involves a screening procedure for kindergarten children to identify those considered to be at risk of developing conduct problems in childhood and adolescence. Results support the use of screening measures as a predictor of future conduct problems in that, 70 per cent of the high risk group had problematic outcomes.

12. Botvin, G.J., Baker, E., Dusenbury, L., Botvin, E.M., Diaz, T. (1995). Long-term follow-up

results of a randomised drug abuse prevention trial in a white middle-class population. *Journal of the American Medical Association* **273**: 1106–1112.
The main focus of the intervention was the provision of information and teaching skills for resisting social influences to use drugs as well as generic personal and social skills for increasing overall competence in young adolescents. Students were taught cognitive-behavioural skills for building self esteem, resisting advertising pressure, managing anxiety, communicating effectively, developing personal relationships and asserting rights. These skills were taught using a combination of teaching techniques including demonstration, behavioural rehearsal, feedback and reinforcement, and homework assignments. Outcomes were positive in that alcohol, marijuana and cigarette use was reduced.

13. Horacek, H.J., Ramey, C.T., Campbell, F.A., Hoffman, K.P. & Fletcher, R.H. (1987). Predicting school failure and assessing early intervention with high-risk children. *Journal of American Academy of Child and Adolescent Psychiatry* **26**: 758–763.
The intervention is a school age curriculum programme which consists of a home/school resource teacher for each child and family in the intervention group for the first three years of school. The programme involved the teacher preparing a set of home activities to supplement the school curriculum in mathematics and reading. Parents were taught how to pursue these activities with the child. The intervention proved highly effective in reducing school failure and boosting competence.

14. Hawkins, J.D., Doueck, H.J. & Lishner, D.M. (1988). Changing teaching practices in mainstream classrooms to improve bonding and behaviour of low achievers. *American Educational Research Journal* **25**: 31–50.
The intervention involved changing teaching practices in mainstream classes for greater involvement, learning and success for low-achieving students. The training course for teachers included three main components: proactive classroom management, interactive teaching and co-operative learning. Low achievers in experimental classrooms showed more favourable attitudes to school, better expectations of continuing in school and less serious misbehaviour in school.

15. Ellickson, P.L. & Bell, R.M. (1990). Drug

prevention in junior high: a multi-site longitudinal test. *Science* **247**: 1299–1305.
The project aimed to reduce the use of cigarettes, alcohol and marijuana in young adolescents by helping them to develop reasons not to use drugs, identify pressures to use them, counter pro-drug messages and to learn to say no. The programme curriculum uses question and answer techniques, group exercises, modeling and repeated skills practice. Outcome measures indicate that programme students smoked significantly less. The project also produced modest drinking reductions in students in the three months following the intervention.

16. Rotherham, M.J., Armstrong, M. & Booraem, C. (1982). Assertiveness training in fourth and fifth grade children. *American Journal of Community Psychology* **10**: 567–582.
The intervention is an assertiveness training programme aimed at children aged 10-12. The programme was incorporated into the classroom curriculum. The course involved 24 one hour sessions over a twelve week period. In a session the pupils were presented with a problem situation for which they had to generate and role play solutions. Teacher ratings at one year follow up showed children who had been through the assertiveness training were rated as more popular, with better classroom behaviour and higher achievements.

17. Coie, J.D. & Krehbiel, G. (1984). Effects of academic tutoring on the social status of low-achieving, socially rejected children. *Child Development* **55**: 1465–1478.
A specific programme for teaching reading provided a graduated method of teaching reading skills by building upon skills that the child had already mastered. A similar approach was used to teach maths. The emphasis was on building self confidence in the child. Improvements were demonstrated in both reading and maths for children who had received this extra tuition. Classroom behaviour was also improved.

18. Tremblay, R.E., Vitaro, F., Bertrand, L., LeBlanc, M., Beauchesne, H., Boileau, H. & David, L. (1992). Parent and child training to prevent early onset of delinquency: The Montreal Longitudinal-Experimental Study. In: J. McCord & R.E. Tremblay (Eds). *Preventing antisocial behaviour*. Guildford Press: New York.
The intervention involves parents and teachers of 7-8 year old boys who had been previously

identified as disruptive by teachers. The programme involved training parents to: monitor their children's behaviour; give positive reinforcement for prosocial behaviour; punish effectively without being abusive and to manage a family crisis. Parents were also given a reading programme to use with their children. At 3 year follow-up the disruptive boys were less physically aggressive in school, had less social adjustment problems and reported fewer delinquent behaviours.

19. Hawkins, J.D., Catalon, R.F., Morrison, D.M. O'Donnell, J., Abbot, R.D. & Day, L.E. (1992). The Seattle Social Development Project: Effects of the first four years on proactive factors and problem behaviours. In: J. McCord & R.E. Tremblay (Eds). *Preventing antisocial behaviour.* Guildford Press: New York.
This intensive intervention was aimed at children aged 7-11 and consists of three components: (i) classroom teaching practices. Teachers received instruction on maintaining classroom order, providing appropriate encouragement and praise, interactive teaching methods and co-operative teaching methods. (ii) Child skills training. Children were taught how to communicate, make decisions and resolve conflicts. (iii) Parent training to enable parents to monitor behaviour, to help children improve reading and maths skills and to learn to communicate effectively with teachers. The intervention resulted in fewer children initiating delinquency or alcohol use than children in the control group. Children in the intervention group also reported better communication and attachment to family.

20. Kellam, S.G. & Rebok, G.W. (1992). Building developmental and etiological theory through epidemiological based preventive intervention trials. In: J. McCord & R.E. Tremblay (Eds). *Preventing antisocial behaviour.* Guildford Press: New York.
This intervention involves two programmes: the mastery learning programme designed to strengthen reading skills, and the good behaviour game which is a team-based management strategy that promotes co-operative behaviour in both shy and aggressive children. The good behaviour game resulted in a reduction in aggressive and shy behaviour and the mastery learning intervention improved reading skills in low achieving boys.

21. Pentz, M.A., Dwyer, J.H., MacKinnon, D.P., Flay, B.R., Hansen, W.B., Wong, Y.I., & Johnson,

C.A. (1989). A multi-community trial for primary prevention of adolescent drug abuse. *Journal of the American Medical Association* **261:** 3259–3266.
The programme consists of: skills training in how to resist drugs, correcting beliefs about drug use, recognition of media influences and peer pressure, as well as practice in problem solving. Homework sessions involved parents and family members considering family roles on drug use and successful techniques for avoiding drug use. Results show that the prevalence rates for cigarettes, alcohol and marijuana were reduced following the programme.

22. Hansen, W.B. & Graham, J.W. (1991). Preventing alcohol, marijuana and cigarette use among adolescents: Peer pressure resistance training versus establishing conservative norms. *Preventive Medicine* **20:** 414–430.
The programme consists of four sessions in which information is given about the social and health consequences of using alcohol and other drugs, and five sessions to correct erroneous perceptions of the prevalence and acceptability of alcohol and drug use and to establish a conservative normative school climate regarding substance abuse. Outcome measures showed a decrease in alcohol, marijuana and cigarette use, and showed a reduction in problems resulting from alcohol use.

23. Pedro-Carroll, J.L. & Cowen, E.L. (1985). The Children of Divorce Intervention Programme: An investigation of the efficacy of a school-based prevention programme. *Journal of Counselling and Clinical Psychology* **53:** 603–611.
This is a school based intervention consisting of 10 sessions which focused on clarifying children's misconceptions about divorce, developing cognitive skills, anger expression and control as well as the development of coping skills. Positive outcome measures were shown on variables such as peer sociability, frustration tolerance and adaptive assertiveness. There was also a decrease in feelings of self blame.

24. Bry, H.B. (1982). Reducing the incidence of adolescent problems through preventive intervention: one and five year follow-up. *American Journal of Community Psychology* **10:** 265–276.
The school based programme in which daily attendance and discipline referrals of the students involved were recorded on weekly 'report cards'. Group sessions allowed discussion of the report cards of each student. Positive teacher ratings

were praised, negative ratings led to further discussions on how the student could improve teacher ratings. Students accumulated points for positive ratings over a yearly period to earn a school trip chosen by themselves. At one year follow-up reports of serious school based problems were significantly lower for intervention students.

25. Sandler, I.N., West, S.G., Baca, L., Pillow, D.R., Gersten, J.C., Rogosch, E., Virdin, L., Beals, J., Reynolds, K.D., Kallgren, C., Tein, J.Y., Kreige, G., Cole, E. & Ramires, R.(1992). Linking Empirically based Theory and Evaluation: The Family Bereavement Program. *American Journal of Community Psychology* **20:** 491–523.
The intervention is designed to improve the family response to the death of a parent and the effects on the mental health of children. The intervention consists of: (i) family grief workshops to unite families with similar experiences and to facilitate discussions of grief related experiences between parents and children. (ii) family advisor programme targeting specific mediators for change including parent demoralisation, parental warmth, stable positive events and negative stress events. The programme was found to increase parental perceptions of warmth in their relationships with their children and more satisfaction with their social support.

26. Olweus, D. (1991). Bully/victim problems among school children: Basic facts and effects of an intervention program. In: K. Rubin & D. Pepler (Eds). *The development and treatment of childhood aggression.* Lawrence Erlbaum Associates: Hillsdale, N.J.
There were four basic components to this intervention: A detailed information booklet; a four page folder with information and advice for parents of victims and bullies; a video showing two case histories of bullied children; and a short questionnaire to obtain data about bully/victim problems in schools and the readiness of students to be involved in producing change. The intervention led to many positive effects such as a marked reduction in the levels of bully/victim problems. Antisocial behaviour such as vandalism, theft and truancy was also reduced.

27. Bierman, K.L. (1986). Process of change during social skills training with preadolescents and its relation to treatment outcomes. *Child Development* **57:** 230–240.
This social skills training programme was developed to improve social interactions with peers by encouraging prosocial behaviour and communication skills. The programme consisted

SELECTED REFERENCES – EFFECTIVENESS

of ten half hour sessions in which the target children were paired with two socially accepted, same sex partners from their classroom. Children were trained to develop conversational skills, such as self expression, questioning and leadership (giving advice, suggestions and invitations). Children who participated in the social skills training made more frequent use of conversational skills and received more positive peer support.

Programmes directed at adults

28. Markman, H.J. Penik, M.J. Floyd, F.J., Stanley, S.M. & Clements, M. (1993). Preventing marital distress through communication and conflict management training: A 4 and 5 year follow-up. *Journal of Consulting and Clinical Psychology* **61:** 70–77.
The intervention is a relationship enhancement programme orientated towards preventing problems from developing in couples' relationships rather than focusing on current problems. Couples learnt a set of skills, techniques and principles designed to help them manage negative affect and increase positive communication. (e.g. communication and problem solving skills). Couples practised using the skills while receiving feedback from trained consultants. Outcome measures show, at 4 and 5 year follow up, that couples who participated in the programme were less likely to break up or divorce.

29. Bloom, B.L., Hodges, W.F., Kern, M.B., McFaddin, S.C. (1985). A preventive intervention programme for the newly separated: Final evaluations. *American Journal of Orthopsychiatry* **55:** 9–26.
The six month intervention was designed to provide social support and to facilitate competence building in five areas of concern: socialisation, child rearing and single parenting, career planning and employment, legal and financial issues, and housing. The programme staff provided advice in group sessions or in individual consultations. Staff also played an active outreach role, helping to develop opportunities for social interaction and making appropriate referrals to appropriate agencies. Outcome measures at 30 month follow up demonstrated positive effects on relationships, health, job satisfaction and financial situation.

30. Munoz, R.F. & Ying, Y.W. (1993). *The prevention of depression.* Johns Hopkins:
Baltimore.
The aim of this programme was to prevent depression in Spanish speaking women attending primary care services in San Francisco. The intervention consisted of eight 2 hour weekly sessions, these focused on: the relationship between thoughts and feelings; how thoughts influence mood; how activities affect mood; increasing pleasant activities; social relationships; and planning for the future in thinking preventatively. Significant benefits were shown at one year follow up, measured by the Beck Depression Inventory.

31. Vega, W.A., Valle, R., Kolody, B. & Hough, R. (1987). The Hispanic Network Preventive Intervention Study. A community-based randomised trial. In Munoz, R.E. (Ed): *Depression prevention: research directions.* pp. 217-234 Hemisphere Publishing: Washington DC.
This is a peer group intervention organised and led by identified natural helpers found in the low income communities of Southern California. The intervention is aimed at preventing depression in low income middle aged women (35-50 years) of Mexican descent. Twelve sessions focused upon ways of coping with life events and unanticipated stressful circumstances. Significant effects were shown for women with medium levels of depression.

32. Toseland, R.W., Rossiter, C.M. 7 Labrecqu, M.S. (1989). The effectiveness of peer-led and professionally led groups to support family caregivers, *The Gerontologist* **29:** 465–471.
Peer led groups met for a total of eight weekly, two hour sessions with a focus upon sharing stressful experiences, discussing coping strategies, as well as the provision of support and understanding. Professional support was provided to peer leaders. Outcomes were positive in the peer-led group with reductions in feelings of guilt, worry and self blame.

33. Leff, J., Kuipers, L., Berkowitz, R. & Sturgeon, D. (1985). A controlled trial of social intervention in the families of schizophrenic patients: two year follow-up. *British Journal of Psychiatry* **146:** 594–600.
The intervention consisted of three main components: A short educational programme of two sessions on the aetiology, symptoms, course and management of schizophrenia; a relatives support group; and family sessions which included the patient and were held at home. The relapse rate in the intervention group were much lower than that of the control group.

34. Vachon, M., Lyall, W., Rogers, J., Freedman-Letofsky, K. & Freeman, S. (1980). A controlled study of self help intervention for widows. *American Journal of Psychiatry* **137:** 1380–1384.
This is a peer-led intervention offering support to the newly widowed. Training for the supporters covered bereavement problems, provision of supportive counselling and identification of resources likely to be helpful to new widows. Initially the newly widowed were offered one to one support, including supportive telephone calls as well as practical help in locating community resources. Small group meetings were also available. Outcome measures on variables such as mental health were positive at six month, one year and two year follow up.

35. Heaney, C.A. (1991). Enhancing social support at the workplace: Assessing the effect of the caregiver support programme. *Health Education Quarterly* **18:** 477–494.
This caregiver support programme has three main objectives that relate to the quality of work relationships: (i) To increase the frequency of social interactions between caregivers; (ii) To increase the amount of social support exchanged between caregivers; and (iii) To reduce social undermining among caregivers to enable participants to benefit from the joint problem-solving that characterises a successful support group. Evidence shows that the Caregiver Support Programme was effective in increasing the number and improving the quality of social interactions.

36. McCann, L. & Holmes, D. (1984). Influence of aerobic exercise on depression. *Journal of Personality and Social Psychology* **46:** 1142–1147.
The intervention aimed to decrease depression in female participants and enable them to deal effectively with the stresses in their lives. The programme consists simply of aerobic exercise. Participants were enrolled in a rhythmical aerobic class for one hour twice a week to develop aerobic capacity through strenuous dancing, jogging and running. They were also expected to participate in exercise outside the class. Positive benefits resulted from the programme including a reduction in depression.

37. Vinokur, D., Ryn, M.V., Gramlich, E.M. & Price, R.H. (1991). Long term follow-up and benefit-cost analysis of the Jobs Program: A preventive intervention for the unemployed. *Journal of Applied Psychology* **76:** 213–219.
This preventive intervention for the unemployed was designed to enhance job seeking confidence, increase motivation and reduce the negative feelings that often accompany rejection and disappointments in the job seeking process. The programme was implemented over eight 3 hour sessions which focused on job seeking skills, finding and initiating job leads, preparation of a CV, sharing information and rehearsing job interviews. The intervention participants found jobs more quickly, had higher job seeking confidence with increased motivation than the participants in the control group, and they were more likely to be better paid with more job stability.

38. Hersey, JC., Kilnamoff, L.S., Lam, D.J., Taylor R.L. (1984). Promoting social support: the impact of California's 'Friends can be good medicine' campaign. *Health Education Quarterly* **11** (3): 293–311.
The study by Hersey et al (1984) undertaken in 6 county areas in California used mass media for a more focused mental health goal of providing education about the role of supportive relationships in promoting health and encouraging people to make more of an investment in their relationships with others. The media were complemented by community activities and the evaluation compared 3 campaign approaches: media plus community activity, media only; community activity only. The campaign had a measurable impact on knowledge, attitudes, behavioural intentions and support enhancing behaviours which were maintained over the course of a year.

39. Abbot, M.W., Raeburn, J.M. (1989). Superhealth: a community based health promotion programme. *Mental Health in Australia* **2** (1): 25–35.
Superhealth (Abbot and Raeburn 1989) is a New Zealand general health promotion programme which is underpinned by a holistic model of health promotion. Superhealth Basic, the subject of the reported evaluation, focuses on three moderators of optimal health: coping skills, social support and social and health skills. Participants in the programme set up three personal lifestyle changes and also take part in sessions on healthy eating, exercise and relaxation and stress management skills. The evaluation was concerned to compare an information based with a behaviourally based approach to delivering the programme. While some success was achieved with the information approach gains were significantly greater with the behavioural approach for all global measures. No longer term follow up has yet been reported. The results obtained have been seen as justifying national dissemination. The intervention is low cost and underpinned by a holistic and positive model of health promotion.

40. King, A.C., Taylor, C.B., Haskell W.L. (1993). Effects of differing intensities and formats of 12 months of exercise training on psychological outcomes in older adults. *Health Psychology* **12** (4): 292–300.
There is a growing interest in the psychological benefits of exercise and the study by King et al (1993) provides some useful evidence. Three different formats for undertaking exercise were included in the intervention which took place over 12 months with adults in the 50-64 age group: group based; high intensity home based; lower intensity home based with the control undertaking normal activity. All exercisers reported significantly lower stress and anxiety at 12 months but no differences on depression were recorded between exercisers and controls. There were no significant differences according to the format of the exercise. The results suggest that exercise frequency and sustainability are more important than format and intensity for mental health with this age group.

41. Singer, G.H.S., Irvin, I.K., Irvine, B., Hawkins, N., Cooley, E. (1989). Evaluation of community-based support services for families of persons with developmental disabilities. *Journal of the Association of Persons with Severe Handicaps* **14** (4): 312–323.
This study evaluated the effectiveness of a package of family support services delivered in two forms for families of children with developmental disabilities. The intervention was designed to increase coping skills, use of social support and decrease potential symptoms of anxiety and depression. The intervention was provided in an intensive support group format and a less intensive format. The former included case management, 3 hours respite care a week, assistance from community volunteers and 16 weekly 2 hour classes on coping skills plus opportunities to focus on individual problems in breaks in the sessions. The less intensive format included the case management and 3 hours a week respite care for 16 weeks. The study reported differential impacts on mothers and fathers. Mothers in the intensive support (IS) group showed reductions in stress and anxiety which were maintained over a year.

42. Elliott, S.A., Sanjack, M., Leverton, T.J. (1988). Parents group in pregnancy. A preventive intervention for postnatal depression? In: Gottleib, B.D. *et al.* Marshallling social support: formats, processes and effects. Beverly Hills, California.
This intervention consisted of 11 monthly group meetings beginning from the 4th month in pregnancy and continuing until 6 months postnatal. The sessions had information and social support functions. The early sessions were structured around specific topics but the later ones had no formal agenda. In addition, women received continuity of care from at least one empathic professional and health visitors made one additional visit early in pregnancy to the intervention group parents. Significantly fewer first and second time mothers in the intervention group, when compared with the controls, were diagnosed as depressed in the first two months postnatal. By the third month the differences persisted but were not significant. On self report there were significant impacts on anxiety and depression for the first time mothers, but no differences between groups for the second time mothers.

43. Holden, J.M., Sugovsky, R., Cox, J.L. (1989). Counselling in a general practice setting: controlled study of health visitor intervention in treatment of postnatal depression. *British Medical Journal* **298:** 223-226.
Holden et al determined whether counselling by health visitors was helpful in managing and reducing postnatal depression, where women were identified as depressed at 6 weeks postnatal. This intervention consisted of 8 weekly counselling visits by HV's lasting at least half an hour. There was an emphasis on the importance of listening to clients and encouraging client decision making. Sixty percent of the women in the intervention group compared with 38 per cent in the control group showed no evidence of major or minor illness at the second measurement point. Mothers in the intervention group reported feelings of being supported. Even those in the control group had appreciated the opportunity to talk about feelings during the diagnostic visit.

APPENDIX 2

REFERENCES AND ADDITIONAL LITERATURE

Adams, L. & Holroyd, G. (1989). Promoting mental health. *Health for All News* **8,** Spring, 5–6.

Albee, G.W. (1982). Preventing Psychopathology and Promoting Human Potential. *American Psychologist* **37:** 1043–1050.

Albee, G.W. (1996). Revolutions and counterrevolutions in prevention. *American Psychologist* **51:** 1130–1133.

Albee, G.W., Loffe, J.M. & Dusenbury, L.A. (Eds) (1988). *Prevention, powerlessness and politics.* Sage: London.

Albee, G.W. & Ryan Finn, K.D. (1993). An overview of primary prevention. *Journal of Counselling and Development* **72** (2): 115–123.

Bien, T.H., Miller, R. & Tonigan, S. (1993). Brief interventions for alcohol problems: a review. *Addiction* **88:** 315–336.

Bosma, M.W.M. & Hosman, C.H.M. (1990). *Preventie op Waarde geschat.* Beta: Nijmegen.

Burrell, G. (1992). The organisation of pleasure. In Alvesson M. & Willmott, H. (Eds) *Critical management studies.* Sage: London.

Butterworth, T. (1994). Developing Research Ideas from Theory into Practice, Psychosocial Intervention as a Case Example. *Nurse Researcher* **1:** (4) 78–86.

Caplan, R. & Holland, R. (1990b). What is mental health?: a conceptual framework. In *Report on Mental Health Promotion Conference* (1989). HEA: London.

Department of Health (1995). *The state of the public health - the annual report of the Chief Medical Officer of the Department of Health.* HMSO: London.

Department of Health (1994a). *ABC of mental health in the workplace.* DoH: London.

Downie, R.S., Fyfe, C. & Tannahill, A. (1990). *Health promotion: models and values.* Oxford University Press: Oxford.

Epp, J. (1988). Promoting the mental health of children and youth: Foundation for the future. *Canadian Journal of Public Health* **79**(suppl. 2): S6–S9.

Fernando, S. (1995). 'Mental health promotion: the way forward'. In *National Mental Health Promotion Conference.* HEA: London.

Glover & Kamis-Gould (1996). Performance Indicators in Mental Health Services. In Thornicroft, G. & Strathdee, G. (1996). *Commissioning Mental Health Services.* HMSO: London.

Goldberg, D. & Huxley, P. (1992). *Common mental disorders.* Routledge: London.

Grant, D. & Oswick, C. (Eds) (1996). *Metaphor and organizations.* Sage: London.

Greenoak, J., Lethbridge, J. & Hunt, R. (1994). *Mental health priorities for action.* (unpublished) Health Education Authority document.

Hagard, S. (1988). Is mental health promotion possible? Lecture to the Annual General Meeting of the Cambridgeshire Mental Welfare Association.

Halm J. (1989). Mental health prevention. In Neumann, J., Schroeder, H. & Dresden, P. German Hygiene Museum/Copenhagen: WHO.

Hawe, P., Degeling, D. & Hall, J., (1990). *Evaluating health promotion – a healthworkers guide.* Maclennan & Petty: Sydney.

Health Australia Project (1996). *Building capacity to promote the mental health of Australians* (discussion paper). Health Australia.

Health Education Authority (1990). *National Mental Health Promotion Conference.* HEA: London.

Health Education Authority (1996). *Positive steps: mental health and young people - attitudes and awareness among 11-24 year olds.* HEA: London.

Health Education Authority (1997). *HEA research strategy.* HEA: London.

Health and Welfare Canada (1988). *Mental health for Canadians: striking a balance.* Health Canada.

Hendren, R., Birrell Weisen R. & Orley, J. (1994). *Mental health programmes in schools.* World Health Organization Division of Mental Health: Geneva.

Hodgson, R.J. & Abbasi, T. (1995). *Effective mental health promotion: literature review.* Technical Report No.13. Health Promotion Wales: Cardiff.

Hodgson R.J. & Abbasi, T. (1995). *Mental health promotion: options for Wales.* Health Promotion Wales: Cardiff.

Holland, R. (1981). From perspectives to reflexivity. In Bonarius, R., Holland, R. & Rosenburg, R. (Eds) *Personal construct psychology: recent advances in theory and practice.* Macmillan: London.

Holland, R. (1981). *Self in social context.* Open University: Milton Keynes.

Holland, R. (1991). Reflexive practice and usable theory in family work. *Issues in Social Work Education* **11** (1): 44–61.

Holland, R. (1992). Sanity, necessary complexities and mental health promotion. *Changes* **10** (2): 136-145.

Holland, S. (1988). Towards prevention. In Ramon, S. & Giannichedda, M. (Eds) *Psychiatry in transition.* Pluto: London.

Holland, S. (1989). Women and community mental health – twenty years on. *Clinical Psychology Forum* **22:** 35–37.

Holland, S. (1995). Action and interaction in women's mental health and neighbourhood development. In Fernando, S. (Ed) *Mental health in a multi-ethnic society: a multi-disciplinary handbook.* Routledge: London.

Holroyd, G. (1991). Promoting mental health - The Salford experience. In *Community development and health.* Open University Press: Milton Keynes.

Hosman, C. & Veltman, N. (1994). *Prevention in mental health: a review of the effectiveness of health education and health promotion.* International Union for Health Promotion and Education.

...r, E. (1996). Mental health: is this a
...c health issue? – Presentation to the College
...alth Service Executives, Brisbane. In the
...h Australia Project, *Building capacity to*
...ote the mental health of Australians
...ussion paper).

...ational Conference on Health Promotion
...7). Ottawa Charter for Health Promotion.
...h *Promotion* **1**(4): ii v.

...s, R. (1994). 'Principles of Prevention' In
...el, E.S. & Jenkins, R. (Eds) *Prevention in*
...iatry. Gaskell - Royal College of
...iatrists: London.

...s, R. (1997). 'Nations for Mental Health'
...cial *Psychiatry and Psychiatric Epidemiology*
...309-311.

...s, R. (1997). 'The importance of mental
...h and its promotion' (unpublished).

...rt et al, (1996) *Mental health promotion:*
...me is now. Health Canada.

...edy, A. (1988). *Positive mental health*
...otion: fantasy or reality? Greater Glasgow
...h Board Health Education Department:
...ow.

...on, M.J. (1989). Mental health vs. mental
...: A philosophical discussion. *Health*
...ation April/May, 40-42.

...o, M.K. & Patel, A. (1997). The cost of
...l health. (unpublished) Health Education
...rity document.

...on, A.H. (1987). Primary prevention of
...iatric disorders. *Acta Psychiatrica*
...dinavica Supplement 337, 7-13

...onald, G. (1994). Promoting mental?
...h. (unpublished) Health Education Authority
...ment.

...w, A.H. (1968). *Towards a psychology of*
... Van Nostrand: New York.

...rd, J. & Tremblay, R.E. (Eds) (1992).
...nting antisocial behaviour: interventions
...birth through adolescence. Guildford: New

Mental Health Foundation (1997). *Knowing our own minds.* MHF: London.

Moore, T.J., (1991). *A survey of the impact of health promotion within mental health nursing.* University of Wales: Cardiff.

Mrazek, P.J. & Haggerty, R.J. (Eds) (1994). *Reducing risks for mental disorders.* National Academy Press: Washington D.C

Munoz, R.F. & Ying, Y.W. (1953). *The prevention of depression: research and practice.* John Hopkins University Press: Baltimore MD.

Newton, J. (1988). *Preventing mental illness.* Routledge & Kegan Paul: London.

Newton, J. (1992). *Preventing mental illness in practice.* Routledge & Kegan Paul: London.

NHS Centre for Review & Dissemination (1997). *Effective health care: mental health promotion in high risk groups.* University of York.

Paykel, E.S. & Jenkins, R. (Eds) (1994). *Prevention in psychiatry.* Gaskell - Royal College of Psychiatrists: London.

Perlmutter, F.D. (Ed). *Mental health promotion and primary prevention.* Jossey-Bass: San Francisco, CA.

Price, R.H., Cowen, E.L., Lorion, R.P. & Ramos-McKay, J. (1988). *Fourteen ounces of prevention. a casebook for practitioners.* American Psychological Association: Washington DC.

Rawson (1992). The growth of health promotion theory and its rational reconstruction – lessons from the philosophy of science. In Bunton, R. & MacDonald, G (Eds) *Health promotion disciplines and diversity.* Routledge: London.

Rogers, A., Pilgrim, D. & Latham, M. (1996). *Understanding and promoting mental health: a study of familial views.* HEA: London.

Shaffer, D., Enzer, N. & Phillips, I. (Eds) (1989). *Prevention of mental disorders alcohol and other drug use in children and adolescents.* US Department of Health and Human Services: Washington D.C.

Society for Health Education and Promotion Specialists (1997). *Ten elements of mental health, its promotion and demotion : Implications for practice.*

Stakes (1997). Promotion of mental health on the European agenda (first draft document).

Sundberg, N.D. (1995). Personal views about mental health promotion: an exercise using three letters. *Journal of Primary Prevention* **15** (3): 303–312.

Tilford, S., Delaney, F. & Vegells, M. (1997). *Review of the effectiveness of mental health promotion interventions.* HEA: London.

Thomas, R. & Corney, R. (1993). The Role of the Practice Nurse in Mental Health: *Journal of Mental Health* **2:** 65–72.

Thornicroft, G. & Strathdee, G. (1996). *Commissioning mental health services.* HMSO: London.

Trent, D.R. & Reed, C. (Eds) (1992). *Promotion of mental health.* Vol. 1 1991. Avebury: Aldershot.

Trent, D.R. & Reed, C. (Eds) (1993). *Promotion of mental health.* Vol. 2 1992. Avebury: Aldershot.

Trent, D.R. & Reed, C. (Eds) (1994). *Promotion of mental health.* Vol. 3 1993. Avebury: Aldershot.

Trent, D.R. & Reed, C. (Eds) (1995). *Promotion of mental health.* Vol. 4 1994. Avebury: Aldershot.

Trent, D.R. & Reed, C. (Eds) (1996). *Promotion of mental health.* Vol. 5 1995. Avebury: Aldershot.

Tudor, K. (1996). *Mental health promotion: paradigms and practice.* Routledge: London.

Wilson, J.Q. & Lowry, G.C. (Eds) (1987). *From children to citizens: families, schools and delinquency.* Springer-Verlag: New York.

World Health Organization Division of Mental Health (1994). *'Lani' Strip Cartoons for mental health Promotion in the mass ,media.* World Health Organization: Geneva.

APPENDIX 3

HISTORY OF THE PROJECT

In 1994, the Health Education Authority commissioned a study to research evaluation methods used in mental health promotion. It found that 'the traditional health promotion planning model where project goals are derived from a rigorous assessment of need is not being followed in the field of mental health promotion... help is needed for both commissioners and providers in getting through the minefield to come up with a clear and appropriate rationale for mental health promotion work.'(MacDonald, G, 1994). This document helped to shape the thinking behind what became known as the 'Mental Health Core Indicators Project'.

The project began two years later, in April 1996, when funding was secured from the Department of Health. The HEA brought together a small group of people involved in mental health promotion to advise and oversee the work. (Full advisory group membership list outlined in Appendix 4).

The first consultation process was carried out in the autumn of 1996 by a wider group of people interested in mental health promotion. (Full list of participants at the consultation events outlined in Appendix 5). The interests and background of the group were wide ranging, with people from self help and user groups, health promotion providers and academic and teaching services.

A pilot guide was drafted as a result of three, two-day workshops, with further submissions of examples of good practice. The guide was compiled by Laurann Yen, a fellow at the Office of Public Management, and the facilitator of the final two events. The chapter on effectiveness and the additional literature section were drafted by Professor Ray Hodgson, a member of the project's advisory group. The pilot quality framework was launched in April 1997.

The pilot guide was distributed through the HEA's mental health database and was presented at HEA mental health briefing days and a number of national and international conferences. Feedback forms were included in the guide to provide general comments on the content and style of the guide. There was also a small scale qualitative research project completed by Mary Hainge and Greg Rowland. This evaluation made detailed recommendations for the further development of the guide and comments on how it was being used.

This current document *Mental health promotion: a quality framework* is the final product of this project launched on World Mental Health Day, 10 October 1997.

APPENDIX 4

ADVISORY GROUP MEMBERS

Deborah Loeb
Principal Health Promotion Adviser
Community Relations and Health Promotion,
East London & the City Health Authority

Glenn MacDonald
Course Director – Postgraduate Diploma MSc in Health Promotion
Faculty of Health and Social Sciences
University of Central England

Dr Andrew McCulloch
Principal
Andrew McCulloch Associates

Dr Rachel Jenkins
Director
WHO – UK Mental Health Office
Institute of Psychiatry

Prof Ray Hodgson
Director
Cardiff Addiction Research Unit

Ray Holland
Senior Lecturer
King's College

Peter Wilson
Director
Young Minds

PARTICIPANTS AT THE CONSULTATION EVENTS

Russell Caplan
Project Officer – Mental Health,
Health Education Authority

Alison Cobb
Policy Officer, MIND

Chris Dodd
Independent Health Promotion Specialist,
Staffordshire

Rachel Dutton
Project Officer – Mental Health,
Health Education Authority

Dr Jessie Earle
Senior Registrar, Child and Adolescent
Psychiatry, St George's Hospital

Jane Field
Steering Group Member,
Croydon Mental Health Users' Group

Dr Lynne Friedli
Account Manager – Mental Health,
Health Education Authority

Elizabeth Gale
Project Manager – Mental Health,
Health Education Authority

Wendy Gale
Assistant Health Promotion Manager/Specialist
Co-ordinator Mental Health Promotion,
Leeds Health Promotion Service

Gloria Gifford
Mental Health Project Worker,
Brent Mental Health User Group

Gay Gray
Project Officer,
WHO Project – Promoting Mental and Emotional
Health in the European Network of Health
Promoting Schools
Senior Visiting Fellow/Psychotherapist,
University of Southampton

Amorel Heatlie
Student Counsellor

Emma Hogg
Senior Health Promotion Officer, Mid Anglia
Community Health NHS Trust Health Promotion
Service

Ray Holland
Senior Lecturer, King's College

Dominic Lennon
Head of Corporate Marketing, MIND

Alan Levy
Consultant Child and Adolescent Psychotherapist
– Head of Service,
Northwick Park & St Mark's Hospital NHS Trust

Deborah Loeb
Principal Health Promotion Adviser,
Community Relations and Health Promotion,
East London and the City Health Authority

Dr Gordon MacDonald
Academic/Senior Tutor,
University College of Ripon & York, St John

Dr Wolf Markham
School of Education,
University of Birmingham

Dr Andrew McCulloch
Principal,
Andrew McCulloch Associates

Louise Rees
Project Officer – Mental Health,
Health Education Authority

Wendy Sim
Chair Elect,
Association for Student Counselling
Student Counsellor, University of Portsmouth

Carolyn Syverson
Primary Care Development Officer,
Carers National Association

Mary Tidyman
Project Manager – Mental Health,
Health Education Authority

Hazel Trotter
Deputy Director,
Brent and Harrow Health Promotion

Jackie Wilkinson
Director of Caller Services,
The Samaritans

USEFUL NATIONAL ORGANISATIONS WORKING TO PROMOTE MENTAL HEALTH

Health Education Authority
Mental Health Team
Hamilton House Mabledon Place
London WC1H 9TX
0171 413 1991

Manic Depression Fellowship
8-10 High Street Kingston upon Thames
Surrey KT1 1EY
0181 974 6550

Mental Health Foundation
37 Mortimer Street London W1N 8JU
0171 580 0145

Mental Health Media
356 Holloway Road London N7 6PA
0171 700 8129

Mind
Granta House 15-19 Broadway
Stratford   London E15 4BQ
0181 519 2122 (office)
0181 522 1728/0345 660163
(Mind info line 9.15am–4.45pm Mon-Fri)

National Schizophrenia Fellowship
28 Castle Street
Kingston upon Thames Surrey KT1 1SS
0181 547 3937 (office)
0181 974 6814
(advice line 10am-3pm Mon-Fri)

Sainsbury Centre for Mental Health
134-138 Borough High Street London SE1 1LB
0171 403 8790

Young Minds
2nd Floor102-108 Clerkenwell Road
London EC1M 5SA
0171 336-8445 (office)
0345 626376 (parents information service)